CW00816158

Published by Atmosphere
Willis Vean
Mullion Cornwall TR12 7DF
England
Tel 01326 240180

All images Copyright Bob Croxford 2008
Book Design and typography by Bob Croxford Copyright Atmosphere 2008
Printed and bound in Italy

ISBN 978-0-9550805-4-8

Many of the pictures in this and other Atmosphere books are available as large photo prints to frame. For details of sizes and prices see www.atmosphere.co.uk/prints.html

Cover picture: THE SPINNAKER TOWER.

Frontispiece: Close-up of a flower border at SOUTHS

PORTSMOUTH

Portsmouth is a busy, bustling city built on an island. Although it has a venerable history, modern developments are not out of place here.

There were small settlements in the inlets around Portsmouth in pre-Roman times but these numbered no more than a couple of hundred people. We can assume they preferred the shelter of the inland waterways and lagoons for fishing and the clear springs from the South Downs for their water. There is no mention of Portsmouth in the Doomsday Book. When Richard The Lionheart returned to England in 1194 he summoned an army and fleet to Portsmouth and in that year granted the town its first Royal Charter.

It was war which led to the development of Portsmouth as we now know it. During the reign of King John the origins of a permanent naval base and docks supported his attempts to invade Normandy. In the following centuries war with France was a constant theme. Portsmouth became a natural target for French attacks and the mouth of the harbour was fortified in 1418 by Henry V. A hundred years later Henry VIII rebuilt the fortifications in stone and added Southsea Castle to the defences.

The glory and tragedy of naval battles was brought home to Henry VIII in 1545 when he witnessed the loss of his magnificent vice-flagship. The Mary Rose sank off Southsea with the loss of 500 lives while sailing from an engagement with the French fleet in The Solent.

By the time Britain was protecting itself against invasion by Napoleon I of France, Portsmouth had developed into a great naval port and dockyard. The Admiralty in London had become the most diverse, complex and powerful organisation in the world. Mail coaches raced between London and Portsmouth carrying orders, dispatches and navy officers in an almost continuous relay. The organisation of the battle fleet under Horatio Nelson's command was an immense undertaking but one for which Portsmouth was expressly suitable.

There is a very good description of how the HMS Victory crew was chosen. So many wanted to join the ship that Nelson's officers arranged feats of strength and stamina on the Portsmouth quayside. They competed because of the expectation of prize money. The crew was a mixed bunch which curiously

included members from land-locked Switzerland as well as the United States and West Indies. Alongside the 441 English on board were 64 Scots, 63 Irish, 21 Americans, 18 Welsh, 9 West Indians, 7 Dutch, 6 Swedes, 4 Italians, 4 Maltese, 3 Norwegians, 3 Germans, 3 Shetlanders, 2 Channel Islanders, 2 Swiss, 2 Portuguese, 2 Danes, 2 Indians, one Russian, one Brazilian, one African, one Manxman and 3 French.

Nelson's flagship, HMS Victory, was launched in 1765 and saw active service until 1812. Laying at Portsmouth as a signalling school she was in very poor condition when a campaign to save and restore her was started in 1921. In 2005, at the anniversary of the Battle of Trafalgar the ship was in better condition than it had been for 200 years.

Nelson's victory at Trafalgar had a profound effect on history. With supremacy at sea Britain was able to control shipping worldwide. This gave Britain the strength, after the anti slave trade Act of 1807, to form an anti-slavery squadron based in Portsmouth with a station in West Africa. By 1865 nearly 150,000 enslaved Africans had been freed through anti-slavery operations by the Royal Navy and many sailors had given their lives to end the slaves' suffering. Boarding disease-ridden slave ships posed dangerous risks of infection and the unfamiliar climate was similarly unhealthy. Many sailors died from the tropical diseases which were common on the squadron, including dysentery, yellow fever and malaria.

The historic Naval Dockyards and HMS Victory are open to visitors. Also open is HMS Warrior which was the first iron-hulled, armour-plated warship, built for the Royal Navy and completed in October 1861. Warrior was by far the largest, fastest, most heavily-armed and most heavily-armoured warship the world had ever seen. She, for the first time, combined steam engines, rifled breech-loading guns, iron construction, iron armour, and propeller drive all in one ship.

The Naval Dockyard brought prosperity and expansion to the town. Some fine houses were built and development expanded into Southsea. Portsmouth was a target for German bombers during WW2. Over 80,000 properties received bomb damage which led to extensive demolition and re-building after the war. The first wave of building was uninspired, unlike the ambitious designs of recent years.

The Spinnaker Tower, whose elegant shape is based on a spinnaker sail full of wind, is the tallest accessible structure in the country outside London. At 170 metres above sea level the tower gives spectacular views of the city and surrounding countryside. It is also a highly visible landmark and a striking addition to many views. It rises from the water's edge at Gunwharf Quays and is part of an ongoing restoration and building project.

A vital part of the Navy's strength lay in the Marines who also have a strong presence in the city. The statue of 'The Yomper' at Southsea outside the Royal Marine Museum was made by sculptor Philip Jackson. It is modelled on a photograph of Corporal Peter Robinson yomping to 'Sapper Hill'. Yomp is Royal Marines slang describing a long distance march carrying full kit and stands for 'Your own marching pace'.

Southsea Castle was built in 1544 on the orders of Henry VIII to protect the English and Portsmouth docks from French invaders. During the English Civil War, in 1642, the castle was captured by Parliamentary forces, the only time it was defeated in its long history.

With its sheltered all-weather harbour Portsmouth is a natural base for ferry operations to France. The sea is full of ships of all kinds with boats, ships, hovercraft and hydrofoils leaving for the Isle of Wight in an almost continuous stream.

South Parade Pier has had a checkered history. The original pier was destroyed by fire. The present structure was opened in 1908 and has also experienced fires, most notably in 1974 during the filming of the rock-opera 'Tommy'. It still operates today as a traditional seaside pier.

Portsmouth has a small fishing harbour and market in the Camber area.

Old Portsmouth is an area in the earliest part of the town which was less affected by the Blitz. A few elegant streets of houses surround the Cathedral. What was originally a chapel in the 12th century was expanded and changed until finally consecrated in 1991. A short distance from the elegant part of town a completely different area could be found. In the days when Portsmouth was a port for eastern trade the area known as Spice Island was a dockland area renowned for ale houses, gin palaces and brothels.

Portchester, to the west of Portsmouth, lies at the head of the harbour and was 'Portus Adurni', a fine example of a Roman fort which, with the addition of a Norman keep, became Portchester Castle.

After the bustle of Portsmouth the villages to the east provide a welcome contrast. Hayling Island is a peaceful residential island with a long sweeping beach and characterful beach huts.

Langstone, by the bridge across to Hayling, is a popular spot with two pubs to watch the tide come in and reced.

Emsworth was an important port in earlier times and a centre for oyster fishing. It occupies a sheltered position in the lagoon which makes up Chichester Harbour. It is now a popular place for sailing.

Further into the sheltered backwaters of Chichester Harbour lies the attractive village of Bosham. Pre-dating the founding of Portsmouth the village makes a few significant historic claims. It is thought to be the birth and burial place of King Harold, the last Saxon King of England. He sailed for Normandy from Bosham in 1064 and Bosham Church is depicted in the Bayeux Tapestry which tells of Harold's defeat at the Battle of Hastings in 1066.

A sailing boat glides past the SPINNAKER TOWER.

The SPINNAKER TOWER. at nig

The SPINNAKER TOWER, from the Gosport ferry

The SPINNAKER TOWER, and ship's figurehead at GUNWHARF QUAY

Early morning at GUNWHARF QUAYS with the SPINNAKER TOWE

SPINNAKER TOWER. and old crane at GUNWHARF QUAYS.

A view of SPICE ISLAND from the SPINNAKER TOWER.. BLOCKHOUSE POINT, GOSPORT from the SPINNAKER TOW

SPINNAKER TOWER viewing platform.

HMS WARRIOR at sunset

Ship's figurehead of Admiral Benbow at The PORTSMOUTH HISTORIC DOCKYA

...ip's figurehead modelled on Admiral Nelson.

bow of HMS VICTORY.

A cannon of the type used on HMS VICTORY.

HMS VICTO

The figurehead of HMS VICTORY.

HMS VICTOR

HMS ARK ROYAL on the quayside at PORTSMOUTH DOCKYARD.

The Falklands Memorial 'YOMPER'.

The 'Domus Dei' or ROYAL GARRISON CHURCH.

THE ROYAL NAVAL WAR MEMORIAL on Southsea Comm

TELEGRA[...]
BOWERMAN G.J.H.
BROWN A.E.O.
HEFFERMAN J. DE V.
MC NORVELL J.
RUDD W.H.

BOY TELEGRAPHIST

BATTRICK A.D.
FERGUSON J.H.
LAKING R.
NORSWORTHY L.J.

CH. ENG. RM. ARTIFICER
[...]EAR S.J.

set over SOUTHSEA CASTLE.

Coat of Arms of Charles II over the gate at SOUTHSEA CASTLE.

ST BANK FORT.

weed covered sea defences at SOUTHSEA.

Brittany Ferries ship 'BRETAGNE' leaves PORTSMOUTH for France.

CANOE LAKE at SOUTHSE

Swan Pedaloes on CANOE LAKE

Colouful fishing boats at PORTSMOUTH'S FISHING HARBOUR.

P1007

BROAD STREET on SPICE ISLAND has a number of characterful old build

DICKENS' HOUSE the birthplace of the writer Charles Dickens.

Attractive houses in PORTCHESTER.

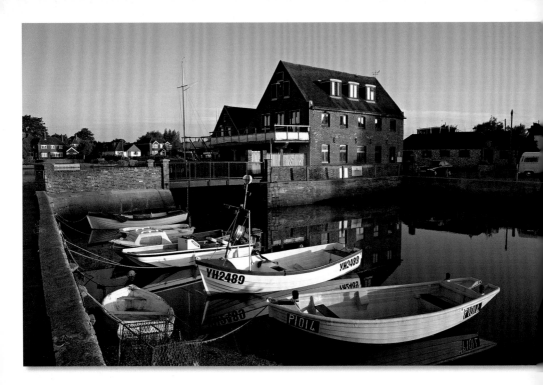

EMSWORTH reflecti

Early morning high tide at BOSHAM.

CHICHESTER HARBOUR at BOSH

INDEX